PROVERBS
FOR LIFE™

for Teachers

inspirio™

Proverbs for Life™ for Teachers
ISBN 0-310-80191-5

Copyright © 2004 by GRQ Ink, Inc.
Franklin, Tennessee 37067
"Proverbs for Life" is a trademark owned by GRQ, Inc.

Published by Inspirio™, The gift group of Zondervan
5300 Patterson Avenue, SE
Grand Rapids, Michigan 49530

Requests for information should be addressed to:
Inspirio™, The gift group of Zondervan
Grand Rapids, Michigan 49530
http://www.inspiriogifts.com

Compiler: Lila Empson
Associate Editor: Janice Jacobson
Project Manager: Tom Dean
Manuscript written by Quentin Guy in conjunction with
    Snapdragon Editorial Group, Inc.
Design: Whisner Design Group

Printed in China.

03 04 05/HK/ 4 3 2 1

Instruct a wise man

and he will be wiser still;

teach a righteous man

and he will add to his learning.

The fear of the Lord

is the beginning of wisdom,

and knowledge of the Holy One

is understanding.

Proverbs 9:9–10 niv

Contents

Introduction

The book of Proverbs contains the timeless wisdom each person needs to live a happy, healthy, well balanced life—each entry teaching a practical principle designed to encourage good choices and positive problem solving.

Proverbs for Life™ for Teachers takes those valuable principles and applies them to the issues you care about most—such as family, health, peace, and commitment. As you read through these pages, may you find the practical answers—God's answers—to the questions you are asking.

The human mind may devise many plans, but it is the purpose of the LORD that will be established.

~ Proverbs 19:21 NRSV

The Fulfilled Teacher

Teach me, good Lord,
To serve you as you deserve.

To give and not to count the cost;

To fight and not to heed the wounds;

To toil and not to seek for rest;

To labor and not ask for any reward

Save that of knowing that I do your will.

Saint Ignatius of Loyola

The Big Day

Reverence for the LORD gives confidence.
~ *Proverbs* 14:26 GNT

Kirsten's heart raced as she stood in front of her first class of high-school freshmen. More experienced teachers had told her to take control immediately or she would have an uphill battle the rest of the year. She tried to tell herself this was no different than her student teaching days. But it was.

The bell had rung, but students were still talking and laughing, shuffling through backpacks, and roaming around the room. She took a deep breath and whispered a prayer. "Lord, this is it—the day I've been preparing for. Please give me confidence."

Kristen scanned the room one more time, and then she was ready, confident that God would give her the strength and courage to do what she knew. "Good morning, everyone. My name is Miss Martin. Would you please take your seats," she announced. Slowly but surely, the chaos came to order.

Accomplishing your dream of becoming a teacher took time and much effort. Meeting the everyday demands of your chosen profession will take even more. Know that you can do it. Know that God is walking right by your side—and that his wisdom, patience, understanding, and peace are yours for the asking. Walk through your school day with confidence, knowing that God is willing and able to supply anything you need to be the teacher he's gifted you to be.

Try this: The day before you face a new challenge, set aside some quiet time to read the Bible and find out what God says about confidence. On an index card, write down Proverbs 3:26 and Hebrews 13:6. Carry them with you as you go to school. Every time you have a free moment, read those verses and pray for God's confidence.

We can say with confidence, "The Lord is my helper; I will not be afraid."

HEBREWS 13:6 NRSV

The Lord will be your confidence.

PROVERBS 3:26 NIV

Only he who can say, "The Lord is my strength," can say, "Of whom shall I be afraid?"

ALEXANDER MACLAREN

Staying the Course

The memory of the righteous will be a blessing.

— *Proverbs 10:7 NIV*

Lynette stared at the stack of ungraded papers in front of her. The students had been gone for more than an hour. She should have finished by now, and she still had four more to go. She had to force herself to read still one more essay with misspelled words, incomplete sentences, and incorrect grammar. It was slow work.

Lynette had spent twenty-two years in the classroom, and she was tired. Had she made any difference at all? Did anyone care? What was the point of her hard work?

Alone in the classroom, she asked God to renew her strength and her sense of purpose. Unexpectedly God brought the smiling faces of some of her former students to mind, and she felt tears springing to her eyes. "Thank you, Lord, for using yesterday's victories to strengthen me for tomorrow's challenges," she whispered.

When you question your effectiveness and wonder if you're making a difference in the lives of your students, call on God. He has walked each and every mile of your journey right along with you. He will bring to mind the faces of students who have conquered geometry, learned to read, overcome shyness, and stayed in school, all because you were there to encourage, instruct, and inspire. Let those memories heal you and help you stay the course.

Try this: In a journal, record the names of those students you feel God has allowed you to help in a special way. Pray for them regularly. And when you hear a bit of good news about one of them, post it in your journal. By keeping track of their successes, you are keeping track of your own.

Let us not be weary in well doing: for in due season we shall reap, if we faint not.

Galatians 6:9 KJV

The path of the righteous is like the light of dawn, which shines brighter and brighter until full day.

Proverbs 4:18 NRSV

When a train goes through a tunnel and it gets dark, you don't throw away your ticket and jump off. You sit still and trust the engineer.

Corrie ten Boom

The Trusting Teacher

It isn't that I cling to Him
Or struggle to be blest;
He simply takes my hand in His
And there I let it rest.

So I dread not any pathway,
Dare to sail on any sea,
Since the handclasp of my Savior
Makes the journey safe for me.

Author Unknown

Trust in the LORD with all your heart and lean not on your own understanding.

~ *Proverbs 3:5* NIV

Blessed are those who trust in the LORD, whose trust is the LORD.

~ *Jeremiah 17:7* NRSV

HOW CALMLY MAY WE COMMIT OURSELVES TO THE HANDS OF HIM WHO BEARS UP THE WORLD.

JEAN PAUL RICHTER

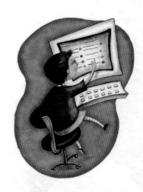

A Better Way

Even children make themselves known by their acts.

~ *Proverbs 20:11 NRSV*

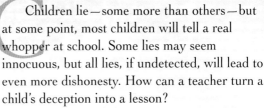

Children lie—some more than others—but at some point, most children will tell a real whopper at school. Some lies may seem innocuous, but all lies, if undetected, will lead to even more dishonesty. How can a teacher turn a child's deception into a lesson?

The best and most positive way to deal with lying is to teach truthfulness. It is reasonable to believe that discerning the difference between the truth and a lie is an acquired skill—something that must be taught.

Look for ordinary opportunities to illustrate truthfulness—even if you are teaching college students. Praise those students who demonstrate honesty, especially when it would seem difficult to do so. Emphasize to your students the rewards of truthfulness—the trust of others, no secrets to cover up, and the confidence that comes from knowing you are pleasing God. For those who've been taught to love the truth, lying is no longer an option.

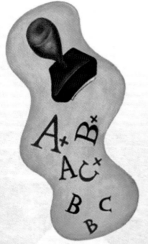

Teaching is much more than standing in front of a classroom with a textbook in your hand. As an effective teacher, you must also strive to make significant contributions to your students' moral education. Ask God to help you find creative ways to communicate the ideal of truthfulness to your students. Help your students reach their full potential by teaching them to recognize the truth and refuse to waver from it.

TRY THIS: *Go to the library or get on the Internet to look for God-honoring ways to teach truthfulness and honesty. Start a file for your research and, at least twice each term, plan a lesson in the form of a story or illustration dealing with truthfulness to present to your students.*

YOU WILL KNOW THE TRUTH, AND THE TRUTH WILL MAKE YOU FREE.

JOHN 8:32 NASB

TRAIN A CHILD IN THE WAY HE SHOULD GO, AND WHEN HE IS OLD HE WILL NOT TURN FROM IT.

PROVERBS 22:6 NIV

Truth is the foundation of all knowledge and the cement of all societies.

JOHN DRYDEN

Tough Questions

The heart of the righteous ponders how to answer.

— *Proverbs 15:28 NASB*

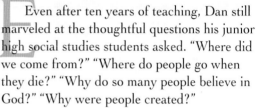

Even after ten years of teaching, Dan still marveled at the thoughtful questions his junior high social studies students asked. "Where did we come from?" "Where do people go when they die?" "Why do so many people believe in God?" "Why were people created?"

These were challenging and tough questions, and school policy about sharing personal views on God made them even more difficult. Dan believed that with God's help he could provide answers that were wise and credible without violating any rules.

"My dad says God doesn't exist. Is that true?" a seventh-grade boy asked one day during a discussion on world events. Dan took a moment to choose his words. Then he answered. "That's a good question," he told the boy, "I suggest that you look around—at the sky, the earth, all of the spectacular beauty and unique creatures—I think that deep down inside, you probably already know the answer."

Jesus was often asked tough questions when he was here on earth, sometimes by his followers and other times by religious leaders who wished to trap him. For each question, Jesus looked to his heavenly Father for a wise and effective answer. Before long, he had gained a reputation as a great teacher. As you look to God, he will also help you give your students the answers they are looking for.

Try this: *Develop the habit of jotting down student questions and comments in the margin of your lesson planner. Then, outside of the classroom, use those notes as a guide for developing wise answers to relevant questions. As time goes by, refer back to those notes to add new insights and understanding on those topics.*

The mediocre teacher tells. The good teacher explains. The superior teacher demonstrates. The great teacher inspires.

WILLIAM A. WARD

Keeping Your Cool

Anger is cruel and fury overwhelming.

~ *Proverbs 27:4* NIV

Mark sighed deeply. He caught himself just as his voice had risen into that you're-making-me-crazy range. He stood before a silent classroom; the tension was palpable. He breathed out slowly and forced a smile. "Sorry, guys. Let's try this again."

Mark loved young people. That was the reason he went into the teaching profession in the first place. Nevertheless, circumstances were always cropping up in the classroom that made it difficult for him to manage his anger and frustration—difficult personality, group dynamics, and fatigue.

As he walked back to his desk, Mark prayed for patience and self-control. *Lord, help me be the teacher you've called me to be. Give me calmness and persistence,* he prayed. "Now," he told his students, "we're going to begin again, and this time, we're going to treat this classroom with the respect it deserves. Learning is a privilege, and it's my job to make sure we all remember that."

If you're accustomed to spending regular, daily time with God, it's easier to turn to him for help when things get crazy at school. Some people have tempers with naturally long fuses; they take forever to burn down. Others have virtually no fuse at all. Either way, God can help you extend your fuse as needed to meet the challenges you must face each day in your classroom.

Try this: *List the types of things that trigger your anger in the classroom. Being knowledgeable about your weak spots will help you prepare in advance to handle situations where anger and frustration threaten to push you over the line. For each trigger on your list, develop and write down a response strategy in advance and commit each one to memory.*

Whoever is slow to anger has great understanding, but one who has a hasty temper exalts folly.

Proverbs 14:29
NRSV

Let everyone be quick to listen, slow to speak, slow to anger; for your anger does not produce God's righteousness.

James 1:19–20
NRSV

He that overcomes his anger conquers his greatest enemy.

Latin Proverb

Places Everyone!

They die for lack of discipline.

~ *Proverbs* 5:23 NRSV

The best discipline, maybe the only discipline that really works, is self-discipline.

Walter Kiechel III

Bus drivers are amazing—they get the kids to school, and it takes a blizzard to stop them. Moreover, they let the kids know who's in charge—there can be only one bus driver per bus. Think of it this way: you're the bus driver in your classroom.

Every day you must be equipped, organized, and geared up. It is up to you to make sure that you're prepared for the day's needs and demands. Your classroom needn't be run with military precision and pace—but without a disciplined tone, you're going to be playing the role of ringmaster rather than bus driver.

Discipline is more about how you teach your students than about what you teach. Discipline is having the wisdom to manage the individual for the benefit of the entire group, and is the ability to pull order from chaos. Depend on God for his help, and pray for ways to obtain the proper tone of discipline for maximum learning.

Ready to go today? Got your copies run, your experiment set up, your small groups handpicked for maximum success? There's more. Discipline begins with discipleship. Spend time in prayer, and spend time gaining insights from God's Word. When you spend that daily time with God—your own personal Bus Driver—praying for the cares of the day and for your success and that of your students, you'll develop the discipline habits that will serve as models for your students.

Try this: Teach your students the benefits of personal discipline by inspecting binders and lockers at least twice a week. Use the time in a positive way to point out simple techniques for keeping things in order—tabbing, file folders, using an assignment book. Be sure to consistently provide a verbal or extra credit award, especially for improvement.

WHOEVER LOVES DISCIPLINE LOVES KNOWLEDGE.

PROVERBS 12:1 NIV

HE WHO HEEDS DISCIPLINE SHOWS THE WAY TO LIFE.

PROVERBS 10:17 NIV

God does not discipline us to subdue us, but to condition us for a life of usefulness and blessedness.

BILLY GRAHAM

The Extraordinary Teacher

To faith add goodness, simply blest,

To goodness, knowledge, beyond the test,

To knowledge, control, put self to rest,

Perseverance follows, lines the nest.

To this, godliness, which shall address

The artless joys of true kindness.

Once under love's domain,

confess That for God's glory

you'll do your best.

CLARK LEGG

Lips that speak knowledge are a rare jewel.

~ *Proverbs* 20:15 NIV

We can do nothing against the truth, but only for the truth.

~ *2 Corinthians* 13:8 NASB

THE QUALITY OF A PERSON'S LIFE IS IN DIRECT PROPORTION TO THEIR COMMITMENT TO EXCELLENCE, REGARDLESS OF THEIR CHOSEN FIELD OF ENDEAVOR.

VINCENT T. LOMBARDI

An Atmosphere of Learning

Those who work for good will find happiness.

~ Proverbs 12:20 GNT

The world is disquieted and uneasy. The global community is divided, and domestic and foreign activities and threats provide daily headlines. In the educational community violence is rampant as never before, and the Prince of Peace has been dismissed from the classroom.

When the world, both inside and outside of school, becomes chaotic and tumultuous, you have an opportunity to make a difference. You serve as a barometer for your students. They watch your response to undue pressure, heavy workloads, and difficult situations in the classroom. They watch your reaction to turmoil in the world. You have many opportunities to show your belief in God and to establish through your own peaceful demeanor that he is in control.

Everything you are as God's child should come through in your teaching. Forgiveness and grace, kindness and compassion, confidence and peace — these gifts are reminders to you, and through you to your students, of God's care.

There is no guarantee that storm clouds will rain on everyone but you. When you're getting soaked like everyone else, peace comes from knowing that you need not rely on what you feel but on what you know. You know that God is there with you through it all and that his love is sure and certain. That peace can never be taken from you.

Try this: Take a few moments during the school day—whether it seems like you need it or not—and find a private place where you can just sit still before God. Give him at least three minutes, more if you can. Turn your thoughts toward your loving Creator, and let him renew your reservoir of peace.

YOU MUST STRIVE FOR PEACE WITH ALL YOUR HEART.

I PETER 3:11 GNT

TO SET THE MIND ON THE SPIRIT IS LIFE AND PEACE.

ROMANS 8:6 NRSV

Peace that Jesus gives is not the absence of trouble, but is rather the confidence that he is there with you always.

AUTHOR UNKNOWN

A Direct Line

The prayer of the upright is his delight.

~ Proverbs 15:8 KJV

IS PRAYER YOUR
STEERING WHEEL
OR YOUR SPARE
TIRE?

CORRIE TEN BOOM

"What's with this day, Lord?" Carolyn mumbled. "How am I going to get myself and my students back on track?" She lifted her head off her desk and glanced around. Dazed by a day that had been derailed by students who argued in the lunch line, passed notes when they were supposed to be doing their math, Carolyn gazed through the window at the third graders at recess playing in the red and orange autumn leaves.

Colors and shapes blended as her mind refocused on a single image: two of the children had ventured up to the window and held a handmade card to the glass. The message was simple: WE LOVE YOU MRS. VANDERWAL! Those few words set her day back on track.

She returned the children's waves and smiles, and off they ran. Her heart in her throat, she whispered, "Thanks, Lord, for your quick and certain answer. I can always count on you."

There's only one way to get a direct line to God—that is by having and maintaining a personal relationship with him. When you're used to talking with him, however briefly or spontaneously, you get used to results—whether they be yes, no, or wait. God is not like a long lost relative, with whom you haven't spoken for years; he is keenly aware of your current situation and is waiting to hear from you so that he can respond to you directly.

Try this: Keep a small journal in your desk drawer to record God's answers to your teaching-related prayers. Be sure your journal has a lock and keep it tucked away out of sight. Record the date, the nature of the prayer, and how God answered. Refer to your journal during the times you need to be reminded that God is never far away.

THE PRAYER OF THE RIGHTEOUS IS POWERFUL AND EFFECTIVE.

JAMES 5:16 NRSV

PRAY IN THE SPIRIT ON ALL OCCASIONS WITH ALL KINDS OF PRAYERS AND REQUESTS. WITH THIS IN MIND, BE ALERT AND ALWAYS KEEP ON PRAYING.

EPHESIANS 6:18 NIV

In prayer it is better to have a heart without words than words without a heart.

JOHN BUNYAN

Making Your Words Count

Pleasant words promote instruction.

~ *Proverbs 16:21 NIV*

Joyce shook her head as she took a second look at Mason's third submission of a simple term-paper assignment. Knowing it was sometimes difficult for seventh graders to be attentive, she had gone over the instructions step by step on the board and had provided a printout for her students to take with them. Then when the papers were in, she had made comments in writing before returning them for revisions.

Mason still wasn't getting it. This would be the second time she had met with him personally. Joyce took a deep breath as Mason shuffled into the room and stood before her desk.

Looking up, Joyce's first impulse was to chastise him for not following instructions, again. But she restrained herself. Instead she asked Mason to sit down. "Okay Mason," she began. "Don't be discouraged. I know you can do this. And I am here to help you do it."

You have a wonderful opportunity to touch a lot of lives. Your students come and go quickly; yet even over the short term your speech and your actions can have a significant impact. Make your words count by seeing that they build up rather than tear down. It's a challenge, because sometimes words of exasperation must first be suppressed. Ask God to help you find the right words for each of your students.

Try this: Sponsor a praise board in or near your classroom. Establish guidelines such as positive words only and privacy respected. Encourage students, teachers, and administrators to contribute on a regular basis. Each month, choose two students to monitor the board. A standard bulletin board is a great way to display simple words of praise, thanks, and encouragement.

LIKE APPLES OF GOLD IN SETTINGS OF SILVER IS A WORD SPOKEN IN RIGHT CIRCUMSTANCES.

PROVERBS 25:11 NASB

DO NOT USE HARMFUL WORDS, BUT ONLY HELPFUL WORDS, THE KIND THAT BUILD UP AND PROVIDE WHAT IS NEEDED, SO THAT WHAT YOU SAY WILL DO GOOD TO THOSE WHO HEAR YOU.

EPHESIANS 4:29 GNT

Kind words also produce their image on men's souls; and a beautiful image it is. They smooth, and quiet, and comfort the hearer.

BLAISE PASCAL

A Spoonful of Sugar

Do not let kindness and truth leave you.

— *Proverbs 3:3 NASB*

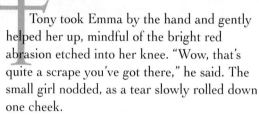

Tony took Emma by the hand and gently helped her up, mindful of the bright red abrasion etched into her knee. "Wow, that's quite a scrape you've got there," he said. The small girl nodded, as a tear slowly rolled down one cheek.

Tony knelt in front of her. "I'll bet that Mark didn't mean to bump you like that. I don't think he saw you." Emma's lip quivered. Tony leaned in and whispered behind his hand, "Sometimes kids act like little chickens. They run around flapping their wings and bumping into each other." He pumped his arms a few times and made a silly, quiet chicken noise. Emma's smile started in her eyes then slowly spread to the corner of her mouth.

"C'mon," said Tony, "Let's go get that scrape cleaned up." Tony cleaned Emma's knee, applied some ointment, and covered it with a special bandage. Then he added two funny stickers to keep the smile on Emma's face.

Think back to the teachers who made the greatest positive impact on your life. It's likely that they all had one common characteristic—they were kind. Showing kindness helps to establish trust and rapport between teacher and student, which often leads to an openness to learning. Even discipline is more effective when it is administered with kindness. As you work on your lesson plans, determined to give your students the best possible learning experience, add kindness to establish the best possible learning environment.

Try this: Develop the habit of purposefully planning at least one act of kindness each day. Bring enough lunch to share with a colleague or leave an anonymous note of encouragement for a student or teacher. Who do you see who might need a candy bar or, better yet, a listener? Ask God to point someone out for you.

WORRY CAN ROB YOU OF HAPPINESS, BUT KIND WORDS WILL CHEER YOU UP.

PROVERBS 12:25 GNT

THEREFORE, AS GOD'S CHOSEN PEOPLE, HOLY AND DEARLY LOVED, CLOTHE YOURSELVES WITH COMPASSION, KINDNESS, HUMILITY, GENTLENESS AND PATIENCE.

COLOSSIANS 3:12 NIV

Be the living expression of God's kindness: kindness in your face, kindness in your eyes, kindness in your smile, kindness in your warm greeting.

MOTHER TERESA

The Joyful Teacher

I have found His grace is all complete,
He supplieth ev'ry need;
While I sit and learn at Jesus' feet,
I am free, yes, free indeed.

I have found the joy no tongue can tell,
How its waves of glory roll!
It is like a great o'erflowing well,
Springing up within my soul.

Barney E. Warren

*Be joyful always;
pray continually; give
thanks in all
circumstances, for this is
God's will for you in
Christ Jesus.*

~ *1 Thessalonians*
5:16–18 NIV

*The prospect of the
righteous is joy.*

~ *Proverbs 10:28* NIV

JOY CAN BE REAL
ONLY IF PEOPLE
LOOK UPON THEIR
LIFE AS A SERVICE,
AND HAVE A
DEFINITE OBJECT
IN LIFE OUTSIDE
THEMSELVES AND
THEIR PERSONAL
HAPPINESS.

LEO TOLSTOY

Before the Bell Rings

I love them that love me; and those that seek me early shall find me.
~ *Proverbs 8:17 KJV*

Let us leave the surface and, without leaving the world, plunge into God.

Teilhard de Chardin

One of the toughest obstacles that you will face as a teacher is finding time to spend with God. You understand the importance of doing so; however, you may find yourself wondering how you're going to fit meditation into your schedule.

When things get really tight, especially around the end of the marking period or when you have a stack of papers to pore over, time devoted to God is usually the first thing to go. The thing is, that time with God may well be the most important thing you do all day. The insights you gain can provide much needed inspiration.

God is the one who placed within you the desire to teach. He's the one who called you to this noble profession and endowed you with gifts and talents. And he is the one who strengthens and motivates you day to day as you spend that important time meditating on his word. You can't afford to do without this time.

Your time spent with God is similar to the time you spend developing relationships with loved ones and friends. You share your thoughts, plans, and feelings, and you want to know theirs. Sometimes it is sufficient simply to enjoy being in the same space. At other times there is more work involved as you study and learn how to know each other better. It's the same with God—only the results are remarkably different.

Try this: You advise your students to set aside a quiet time and place to study; and you should do the same for your quiet time with God. Whether it's your breakfast nook or a nearby coffee shop, treat your time with God as a standing date and keep it. Go expecting that you'll be better for time spent with the one who loves you best.

I study your instructions; I examine your teachings.

PSALM 119:15 GNT

WHATEVER IS TRUE, WHATEVER IS NOBLE, WHATEVER IS RIGHT, WHATEVER IS PURE, WHATEVER IS LOVELY, WHATEVER IS ADMIRABLE—IF ANYTHING IS EXCELLENT OR PRAISEWORTHY—THINK ABOUT SUCH THINGS.

PHILIPPIANS 4:8 NIV

Those who draw water from the wellspring of meditation know that God dwells close to their hearts.

TOYOHIKO KAGAWA

Finding the Answer

The LORD gives wisdom.

— *Proverbs* 2:6 NASB

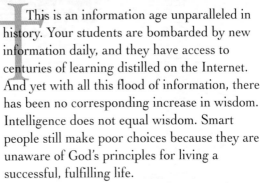

This is an information age unparalleled in history. Your students are bombarded by new information daily, and they have access to centuries of learning distilled on the Internet. And yet with all this flood of information, there has been no corresponding increase in wisdom. Intelligence does not equal wisdom. Smart people still make poor choices because they are unaware of God's principles for living a successful, fulfilling life.

Many schools initiate, with varying degrees of success, programs that focus on developing character. These programs are implicit acknowledgment that knowledge alone — that is, knowledge without wisdom — is insufficient to produce a complete person who is a contributing citizen. As a Christian, you know that true wisdom comes only from God.

Be a light to your students on the path to wisdom. Make wise choices for yourself — keep learning, stay in shape, eat well, come prepared. Demonstrate in as many ways as possible how to effectively use the things your students are learning.

TRUE WISDOM LIES IN GATHERING THE PRECIOUS THINGS OUT OF EACH DAY AS IT GOES BY.

E. S. Bouton

If wisdom were a corollary of age, you'd be retired from teaching before you actually figured it all out. Without God, it's impossible to attain real wisdom, which is attached to eternal values. A broad definition is that wisdom is the application of knowledge to living—what you do (or don't do) with what you know. Many other factors figure in—experience, circumstance, and awareness of ignorance—that your need for God is startlingly clear.

Try this: *Dig into your Bible and get some wisdom—find three verses on wisdom and write them on separate index cards. On the back of each, describe why you chose that particular verse, and how you might apply that wisdom at school. Post them where you'll see them and put a checkmark on each one each time you use that wisdom.*

WISDOM IS THE PRINCIPAL THING; THEREFORE GET WISDOM; AND WITH ALL THY GETTING GET UNDERSTANDING.

PROVERBS 4:7 KJV

IF ANY OF YOU IS LACKING IN WISDOM, ASK GOD, WHO GIVES TO ALL GENEROUSLY AND UNGRUDGINGLY, AND IT WILL BE GIVEN YOU.

JAMES 1:5 NRSV

Never mistake knowledge for wisdom. One helps you make a living and the other helps you make a life.

SANDRA CAREY

A Time to Laugh

A cheerful heart is good medicine.

~ Proverbs 17:22 NIV

Although her colleagues dreaded it, Jessica secretly looked forward to prank week. There was a longstanding tradition of nondestructive, harmless practical joking at her school. God invented humor, and Jessica always enjoyed a hearty laugh. Kids gained as much from teachers who displayed an appropriate sense of humor as from undue seriousness, she reasoned.

She kept a straight face as she walked into her 8:00 A.M. biology class. All looked well until she glanced at the display in front of her. The bulletin board was covered with dissected frog legs stapled to a pattern.

She turned and faced her class, all of whom were doing their very best to maintain sober faces. "Apparently," she said, "someone failed to take the time to teach the freshmen proper dissection technique." A minute later, she held up a hand to lower the level of laughter that had exploded.

"Besides," she demurred, "you guys forgot the deep fryer and the barbecue sauce."

Isn't it wonderful to know that the Bible calls laughter "good medicine"? By sharing a humorous moment with your students, you've connected with them on one of the most fundamental levels possible. Smiles and laughter bridge almost every gap created by culture, religion, socioeconomic status, gender, or age. Gratitude for God's blessings sets the stage for genuine delight in the process of walking with him daily.

Try this: *Create two lists: one of appropriate jokes, puns, riddles, and funny stories to share with your students, and the other of Bible verses that emphasize such themes as joy, gladness, happiness, and good cheer. Use the first to share some laughter and fun, and use the second to remind yourself of God's beautiful gift of joy.*

THE CHEERFUL HEART HAS A CONTINUAL FEAST.

PROVERBS 15:15 NIV

MAY THE RIGHTEOUS BE GLAD AND REJOICE BEFORE GOD; MAY THEY BE HAPPY AND JOYFUL.

PSALM 68:3 NIV

When people laugh together, they cease to be young and old, master and pupils, worker and driver. They have become a single group of human beings, enjoying their existence.

WILLIAM GRANT LEE

Holding the Line

The wise will inherit honor.
~ *Proverbs* 3:35 NRSV

He that respects not is not respected.
George Herbert

As Patricia dialed the Dawsons' number, she tapped her pencil against the table. These phone calls from parents in the middle of the day seldom featured a positive message. And Brandon's history of misbehavior, coupled with his mother's reputation for denial, enabled Patricia to anticipate what would be said. She dreaded that sort of confrontation.

Later that afternoon, Patricia was still shaking her head in amazement at what had actually transpired. Mrs. Dawson wasn't upset at all. Instead, she was quite enthusiastic about Patricia's progress with Brandon. "You've earned his respect somehow, Miss Dickinson. He feels like you're giving him a fair shake and not going on what others may have said about him. I want you to know how much his father and I appreciate your efforts. Please let us know what we can do on our end to help him."

Patricia smiled, thinking about her relationship with God. *Lord, all I know I learned from you.*

42

As a teacher you've got to talk the talk—disseminating information, settling conflict, mediating discussions, and promoting peace. You also know the importance of walking the walk—backing up words with deeds, practicing what you preach, and putting honor above expedience. You'll earn your students' and colleagues' respect as you show them that, as a Christian, you'll live your values and beliefs before you ever have to say a word about them.

Try this: Take time once a week to write a letter to a parent you know who is really putting forth an effort to help his or her child be successful in school. This exercise will encourage the parent and it will also remind you to always respect the role that parents play in your students' education.

A GOOD NAME IS RATHER TO BE CHOSEN THAN GREAT RICHES, AND LOVING FAVOUR RATHER THAN SILVER AND GOLD.

PROVERBS 22:1 KJV

HONOR ONE ANOTHER ABOVE YOURSELVES.

ROMANS 12:10 NIV

Without respect, love cannot go far or rise high: it is an angel with but one wing.

ALEXANDRE DUMAS

The Understanding Teacher

I will not wish thee riches,

nor the glow of greatness,

but that wherever thou go some weary

heart shall gladden at thy smile,

or shadowed life know sunshine for a while.

And so thy path shall be a track of light,

like angels' footsteps

passing through the night.

Inscription on a Church Wall,
Upwaltham, England

Call understanding your intimate friend.

~ *Proverbs 7:4 NASB*

The unfolding of Your words gives light; it gives understanding to the simple.

~ *Psalm 119:130 NASB*

Understanding is the reward of faith. Therefore seek not to understand that you may believe, but believe that you may understand.

Saint Augustine of Hippo

United We Stand

By wisdom a house is built, and through understanding it is established.

— Proverbs 24:3 NIV

Elena sat at her desk, enjoying the sound of the rain against her windows, and reread the letter from Chuck's parents: "We just can't believe what a writer Chuck has become this year." Elena smiled. In August, Chuck had barely been able to string two sentences together. By March, he had submitted a movie review to the school paper.

Elena recalled how surprised Mr. and Mrs. Levine had been when she called to tell them his article had been accepted. She guessed they weren't used to hearing good news about Chuck's schoolwork.

"You've reached him when so many others haven't. It must be the calls home, the encouraging words for Chuck, your frequent communication with us—you've made so much difference!"

Oh no, Lord, Elena thought. *We both know the truth. I made an effort—but you made the difference. And I thank you.*

As safe and comfortable as you make your classroom, and as valuable a learning experience as you provide there, the classroom cannot outweigh the importance of the student's home life. This often results in antagonism between teachers and parents. You can preempt such conflict by focusing on a unified effort with parents to support, aid, and teach their children. If your classroom becomes a home away from home, that's fine. See yourself as the parents' ally in raising moral, productive, and wise kids.

Try this: Each week, invite the parents of one of your students to come to the school and have lunch with you and their child. Use the time to get to know the parents on a personal level. Meeting their parents will help you better understand your students, and it will also help you build a bridge for communication and understanding.

A RIGHTEOUS PERSON'S PARENTS HAVE GOOD REASON TO BE HAPPY. YOU CAN TAKE PRIDE IN A WISE CHILD.

PROVERBS 23:24
GNT

GOD SETS THE LONELY IN FAMILIES.

PSALM 68:6 NIV

What we desire our children to become, we must endeavor to be before them.

ANDREW COMBE

It's the Principal

The wise in heart accept commands.

~ Proverbs 10:8 NIV

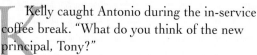

Kelly caught Antonio during the in-service coffee break. "What do you think of the new principal, Tony?"

Tony shrugged. "He's saying all the right things, I suppose, but in fourteen years of teaching, I've heard it all before."

That afternoon, Tony was unpacking and shelving his books when he came across an old leather-bound Bible. He flipped open to a passage where an index card poked through the gold-edged pages. *Romans 13 . . . when did I write this?* He noticed the date on the card—almost exactly two years earlier.

> New principal intro'd today—guy's making some big promises, seems kind of arrogant. Reminder: God is in control. My job—honor the chain of command.

Tony shook his head slowly as his cynicism melted away. He was unable to stand against God's sovereignty. Later, he waved Kelly down. "Hey, Kel—the new guy always deserves a chance, right?"

Kelly stopped, then answered positively with a big smile. "You bet!"

AUTHORITY IS LIKE A BAR OF SOAP—THE MORE YOU USE IT THE LESS YOU HAVE.

JOHN RICHARD WIMBER

The Bible often refers to the importance of authority—God, first and foremost, followed by voluntary submission to bosses, government officials, and so on. It benefits everyone involved—especially your students—when you do everything you can to help those in authority over you succeed. That may mean laying aside some of your own ways of doing things and trying something new. If it works, you will have learned something valuable. Even if it fails, you've gained something—a reputation as someone who honors authority.

Try this: *Carefully read Romans 13, then sketch the chains of command in your school. List the people involved by name; then put the names in order of the decision-making that takes place. Resolve to pray each day for one of the names on your list, starting at the top and working your way down.*

THERE IS NO AUTHORITY EXCEPT THAT WHICH GOD HAS ESTABLISHED.

ROMANS 13:1 NIV

OBEY YOUR LEADERS AND SUBMIT TO THEM, FOR THEY ARE KEEPING WATCH OVER YOUR SOULS.

HEBREWS 13:17 NASB

The first responsibility of a leader is to define reality. The last is to say thank you. In between the leader is a servant.

MAX DEPREE

Failure Isn't Final

Though they fall seven times, they will rise again.

~ *Proverbs* 24:16 NRSV

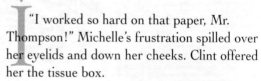

We must accept finite disappointment, but we must never lose infinite hope.

Martin Luther King Jr.

"I worked so hard on that paper, Mr. Thompson!" Michelle's frustration spilled over her eyelids and down her cheeks. Clint offered her the tissue box.

"I know, Michelle," he said gently. "Sometimes you give an assignment everything you've got, and it just doesn't quite work. You've got to keep at it." He remembered his first attempt at his master's thesis—a painful lesson in what not to do and, in the end, what to do.

He held up the paper. "I'm going to do the same thing for you my professor did for me." He ripped Michelle's paper in half and tossed it in the trash can. "That history paper is, well, history. Let's start again. I'll help you pick your topic this time."

"Can we do that?"

"Of course. Michelle, there is always hope. That's the only reason to try and to keep trying."

You will make plenty of mistakes as you walk through your life. If you place your hope in God your life will not be defined by the mistakes you make. With each failure, God will provide an opportunity for you to begin again, to turn things around, and to make good. Your hope will be disappointed only if you decide to give up on yourself, because God never will.

Try this: Make a list of the top three things you are hoping for in life. This may be advancement in your career, a sense of increased satisfaction, or anything else that is important to you. Lay your hand on the list and ask God to help you accomplish those things or to change your perspective concerning them.

There is surely a future hope for you, and your hope will not be cut off.

Proverbs 23:18 NIV

Let us hold unswervingly to the hope we profess, for he who promised is faithful.

Hebrews 10:23 NIV

Hope is not the conviction that something will turn out well but the certainty that something makes sense, regardless of how it turns out.

Vaclav Havel

Praises Given and Received

The lips of the righteous feed many.
— *Proverbs 10:21 KJV*

Betty, a forty-year teaching veteran, stood before the graduating class and the audience of family, friends and colleagues. She had been asked to give the graduation address, and she thanked God for the opportunity.

Smiling, Betty urged the students before her to follow their dreams and never to give up until those dreams became a reality. "And when you reach your goals," she told them, "don't stop there. Reach out yet again, expand your thinking, become more than you hoped you could be."

Afterward, Betty stood with two former students. "The amazing thing," said Chris, "is that what you said today, you have been saying to your students for years. You inspired me to reach farther than I would have thought possible."

"I know your words of inspiration changed my life," Anna, the other former student, confirmed. "And we want to tell you how much we thank God for you. You were God's gift to us when we needed you most."

What if you could live like there was no tomorrow? What would that add to your teaching for the day? Passion? Perspective? Clarity of purpose? Remember: in Christ you have eternal life, but you also have life abundantly here and now. What will inspire your students and colleagues is how you go about today's business, maximizing the good things in your life, the positive aspects of your profession, the joys you receive from teaching.

Try this: Develop the habit of collecting inspirational quotes about teaching from books, magazines, newspapers, and a variety of other sources. Buy an inexpensive photo album and place the quotes under the plastic. When you feel you need inspiration, spend some time looking through your personal quote book.

It is the spirit in a man, the breath of the Almighty, that gives him understanding.

Job 32:8 NIV

The Lord does not see as mortals see; they look on the outward appearance, but the Lord looks on the heart.

1 Samuel 16:7 NRSV

It is not what a man does that determines whether his work is sacred or secular; it is why he does it.

A. W. Tozer

The Patient Teacher

Upward, onward, struggling inward,

Finding grace in spite of sin's words,

Hopeful, thoughtful, sometimes doubtful,

Holding the tongue's a silent mouthful,

Watching, waiting, hesitating,

Then purpose to our actions mating,

Living, longing, not quite belonging,

In our hearts the Spirit's songs sing,

Slaves in perseverance fight,

Patiently chained to God's delight.

Fontrella Nevilles

*It is better to be patient
than powerful.*

~ *Proverbs 16:32* GNT

*Let your hope keep you
joyful, be patient in your
troubles, and pray
at all times.*

~ *Romans 12:12* GNT

With malice
toward none;
with charity for
all; with
firmness in the
right, as God
gives us to see
the right—let us
strive on to
finish the work
we are in.

Abraham Lincoln

THE RIGHT DESTINATION

Train up a child in the way he should go.

~ *Proverbs 22:6 NASB*

"I still don't understand what we're doing here, Mr. Watts."

"I hear you, Adam," said Jim. "But we're not just here today to build a house for a needy family—we're building bridges for families that need help crossing troubled waters in their lives. We are investing in their future and in our own."

"Well, I can see how we're helping them, but I'm not sure how working on someone else's house is going to be important to my future," Adam countered.

"It isn't about houses, Adam. It's about understanding that no one walks into the future alone. We all need each other. Everyone has to be willing to give and receive help. Sometimes you help; sometimes you need to be helped. Your future success depends on learning to do both."

Adam gave that some thought as he and Jim replaced a window and finished painting the kitchen. He liked the idea of using his skills, abilities, and resources in such a needed endeavor.

You've probably read about individuals who pursued their goals for the future with such single-minded determination that they completely disregarded the needs of others and led miserable, lonely lives as a result. Tell your students and show them through your example that the best way to ensure a bright future for themselves is to help others along the way, and to learn early in life to give and receive.

Try this: Spend time talking to your coworkers and colleagues and take note of their dreams for the future. When asked, share your hopes for the future as well. Then find ways to help others on their way. That might mean helping a fellow teacher develop a special curriculum or study for the teacher's proficiency test. Then allow that person to help you in the same way.

THOSE WHO ARE NOBLE PLAN NOBLE THINGS, AND BY NOBLE THINGS THEY STAND.

ISAIAH 32:8 NRSV

THE LORD SAID, "I ALONE KNOW THE PLANS I HAVE FOR YOU, PLANS TO BRING YOU PROSPERITY AND NOT DISASTER, PLANS TO BRING ABOUT THE FUTURE YOU HOPE FOR."

JEREMIAH 29:11 GNT

Even if I knew that tomorrow the world would go to pieces,
I would still plant my apple tree.

MARTIN LUTHER

Nobody Said It Would Be Easy

The righteous cannot be uprooted.

~ Proverbs 12:3 NIV

WHEREAS OBEDIENCE IS RIGHTEOUSNESS IN RELATION TO GOD, LOVE IS RIGHTEOUSNESS IN RELATION TO OTHERS.

Matthew Henry

Garrett had been teaching for years and still struggled with the issue of keeping his relationship with God quiet within the parameters of the classroom. How could he help his students if he couldn't teach what was the most important of all to him—to love and respect God?

Soon after school started one fall, Garrett was invited by another teacher to attend a meeting of Christian teachers that met once a month at a local church. He jumped at the chance to attend and hear what other teachers had to say about the issue.

That night, he boldly asked the question and gained vital perspective. "Words are important, but they aren't the only way to stir a desire to know God in your students. The way you live your life, and your attitudes and behaviors demonstrate God's love," one teacher offered. Garrett recognized the truth of what he said, and thanked God for guiding him to this fellowship.

You face a great number of exciting challenges as a Christian working in the world of education. The challenges are great, and the rewards are even greater. You have the privilege and responsibility of representing the person of Jesus Christ to your students, their parents, and your coworkers on a daily basis. While it may not be possible to talk about your relationship with God in your classroom, you can still find many ways to bring the light of God to your students' lives.

Try this: Choose several students in your classroom for which to pray on a regular basis. Put their names in a prayer notebook at home and pray each day. Ask that God will enlighten them to his presence in their lives and his love for them. Pray for those specific students for an entire term.

WHOEVER PURSUES RIGHTEOUSNESS AND KINDNESS WILL FIND LIFE AND HONOR.

PROVERBS 21:21
NRSV

THE WORK OF RIGHTEOUSNESS SHALL BE PEACE; AND THE EFFECT OF RIGHTEOUSNESS QUIETNESS AND ASSURANCE FOR EVER.

ISAIAH 32:17 KJV

My hope is built on nothing less
Than Jesus' blood and righteousness.
EDWARD MOTE

Hearts Lifted Up

Death and life are in the power of the tongue.

~ *Proverbs 18:21 KJV*

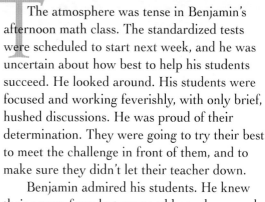

The really great man is the man who makes every man feel great.

G. K. Chesterton

The atmosphere was tense in Benjamin's afternoon math class. The standardized tests were scheduled to start next week, and he was uncertain about how best to help his students succeed. He looked around. His students were focused and working feverishly, with only brief, hushed discussions. He was proud of their determination. They were going to try their best to meet the challenge in front of them, and to make sure they didn't let their teacher down.

Benjamin admired his students. He knew their scores from last year and knew how much they wanted to improve. *There's not going to be an easy question on this test*, he thought. *What they really need is to hear how much I believe in them.*

"Let's take a break, kids," he said to them. I need to tell you a few things before we go on with the lessons."

Scripture frequently emphasizes the value of encouraging words and reminders of what really matters. Those words can mean the difference between failure and success. Your students need more than facts to do well. They also need to know their value as human beings; they need to know that they are more important than any test. When it comes to drawing out the best in your students, your words of encouragement may be the best study aids available to you.

Try this: Learn the art of encouragement by practicing. Set out each morning to speak encouraging words to at least three people during the day. It might be complimenting the principal on her leadership skills or one of your students on a new haircut. When the school day is over, take your encouraging words with you — to the supermarket, the restaurant, the home of a friend.

EVERYTHING THAT WAS WRITTEN IN THE PAST WAS WRITTEN TO TEACH US, SO THAT THROUGH ENDURANCE AND THE ENCOURAGEMENT OF THE SCRIPTURES WE MIGHT HAVE HOPE.

ROMANS 15:4 NIV

OUT OF THE ABUNDANCE OF THE HEART, THE MOUTH SPEAKS. THE GOOD PERSON BRINGS GOOD THINGS OUT OF A GOOD TREASURE.

MATTHEW 12:34–35 NRSV

Expect people to be better than they are; it helps them to become better. But don't be disappointed when they are not; it helps them to keep trying.

MERRY BROWNE

That's Not Fair!

Understand what is right and just and fair.

~ *Proverbs 2:9* NIV

Linda was up to her neck in students, all clamoring to use the one working printer in the computer lab. Suddenly Jason pushed his way through the group to the front of the line. "Let me in—I'm ready to print." Linda gently reminded him that there were others who needed to use the printer as well. He would have to wait his turn. "That's not fair, Mrs. Hendricks—I've been working real hard on this, and I'm finished," Jason said.

Linda explained to Jason—and to all the other listening ears in line—that fairness is more than what is fair for you. Fairness prevails when everyone gets what he or she needs. "You've been working hard, Jason," she continued, "but so has everyone else."

Linda pointed to another student across the room. "If you'll help Steve fix his margins, the time will probably fly by." Jason nodded and went over to Steve.

62

🌿 Justice means giving people what they deserve. This explanation helps children understand that the purpose of justice is to provide peace. Your students look to you for justice—in the way you treat them and in the way you help them treat each other. When the popular notion of I-me-mine is dispensed in favor of the common good, students will make doing the right thing a habit and not just a consequence.

🌿 Try this: *Look up the words just and justice in your Bible concordance. As you read verses where those words are used, put together a definition of what those words mean to God. How does that definition compare to your own ideas about justice? How does God balance his justice with his love and tenderness toward us?*

When justice is done, it brings joy to the righteous.

Proverbs 21:15 NIV

What does the Lord require of you? To act justly and to love mercy and to walk humbly with your God.

Micah 6:8 NIV

Peace is more important than all justice: and peace was not made for the sake of justice, but justice for the sake of peace.

Martin Luther

The Blessed Teacher

God for his service needeth not

Proud work of human skill;

They please him best who labour

Most to do in peace his will:

So let us strive to live,

And to our spirits will be given

Such wings as, when our Saviour calls,

Shall bear us up to heaven.

William Wordsworth

God said, "Blessed are those who keep my ways."

~ *Proverbs* 8:32 NIV

A blessing is what God promised to give you when he called you.

~ *I Peter* 3:9 GNT

THE BEST THINGS ARE NEAREST: BREATH IN YOUR NOSTRILS, LIGHT IN YOUR EYES, FLOWERS AT YOUR FEET, DUTIES AT YOUR HAND, THE PATH OF GOD JUST BEFORE YOU.

ROBERT LOUIS STEVENSON

Planning for Success

The plans of the diligent lead surely to abundance.

— *Proverbs 21:5 NRSV*

It's easier to prepare and prevent than to repair and repent.

Author Unknown

"Is everything ready to go?" The students nodded as Justine gathered them together backstage. They had spent the last six weeks writing, planning, and practicing their own play. Now the excitement of opening night enveloped them—the crowd's loud murmuring, the kids' jittery whispers, and the powerful thumping of Justine's heart.

"When we started, I told you that this would be on your shoulders. If you didn't write the script, it wouldn't get written. If you didn't help make the costumes, they wouldn't get made. If you didn't practice your lines, tonight wouldn't happen." Several heads nodded, reminiscing. Then they waited. She leaned forward and smiled. "You all did what you needed to do. I want you to know, you're ready. Go enjoy your moment."

As she watched from the wings, Justine's heart soared, confident that this would be one of those special events that would mark not only this school year, but these students' entire educational experiences.

You can and should teach organization and preparation. And you should also give your students plenty of opportunities to stand or fall on their own performances. God provided you with opportunities to perfect your faith, and it's the same thing. Teach your students to handle both failure and success, to turn one into the other. That's how you prepare them for life, by closing the gap between the classroom and the world.

Try this: Challenge yourself to better prepare the lessons you present to your students. Before creating your outline, ask yourself the following questions: What specific principle do I want my students to grasp? What illustrations can I draw from my life experience that will illustrate that principle? Do those illustrations demonstrate practical, easy-to-understand applications for that principle?

BE PREPARED IN SEASON AND OUT OF SEASON; CORRECT, REBUKE AND ENCOURAGE—WITH GREAT PATIENCE AND CAREFUL INSTRUCTION.

2 TIMOTHY 4:2 NIV

PREPARE YOUR MINDS FOR ACTION; BE SELF-CONTROLLED; SET YOUR HOPE FULLY ON THE GRACE TO BE GIVEN YOU WHEN JESUS CHRIST IS REVEALED.

I PETER 1:13 NIV

Dig the well before you are thirsty.
CHINESE PROVERB

Raising the Bar

Have not I written to thee excellent things in counsels and knowledge?

— *Proverbs 22:20 KJV*

EVERY JOB IS A
SELF-PORTRAIT
OF THE PERSON
WHO DID IT.
AUTOGRAPH
YOUR WORK
WITH
EXCELLENCE.

AUTHOR UNKNOWN

William flipped through a stack of papers. "Bruce, would you mind staying for just a moment?" Bruce nodded and then stared down at his desktop.

"I noticed I don't have your report." William stated. "Is everything all right?"

Bruce's face reddened; the words seemed stuck in his throat. "I'm sorry, Mr. Kwan. I didn't finish it." William waited. "And you're always telling us that our final product represents our total effort? Well, I just couldn't get it right, and I couldn't turn it in the way it was."

William sighed. "Why didn't you tell me before today? I could've given you extra time."

"It's like you say: a person's ability to meet a deadline reflects his desire to put others' needs before his own. I'll get it to you tomorrow; I promise."

William nodded humbly. "That's fine, son. Remember, excellence isn't about being perfect. It's about always doing your best — you've already gotten that part right."

68

Real excellence is more than top grades and blue ribbons, though these are usually reflective of high standards of diligence and commitment. God is the source of true excellence. True excellence comes when you realize that, despite all of your imperfections and mistakes, God still loves you and has grand designs for your life. Knowing that should inspire you to give your best in all you do, and to encourage your students to the standard of excellence that marks a complete person.

Try this: Every week, recognize moral excellence among your students. When you see them doing the right thing for the right reasons — helping others, saying something kind, defending someone — acknowledge their achievements with a short personal note that describes what you saw them doing. This will inspire them and remind you to look for the right things.

WE HAVE THIS TREASURE IN JARS OF CLAY TO SHOW THAT THIS ALL-SURPASSING POWER IS FROM GOD AND NOT FROM US.

2 CORINTHIANS 4:7
NIV

JESUS SAID, "LET YOUR LIGHT SHINE BEFORE OTHERS, SO THAT THEY MAY SEE YOUR GOOD WORKS AND GIVE GLORY TO YOUR FATHER IN HEAVEN."

MATTHEW 5:16
NRSV

Go first where you would send others, preach Christ without words, demonstrate that virtue and excellence are not ours, but in acting on them we obtain them.

JOHN MARSTON QUESADA

Showing the Way

I guide you in the way of wisdom and lead you along straight paths.

~ *Proverbs 4:11 NIV*

Claudia hoped that this camping trip would be memorable. At every opportunity, Claudia provided tips for a better hiking experience and also opened their eyes and minds to the wonders of being out in God's creation.

At a particularly challenging stream crossing, she taught them how to probe for water depth and how to determine which rocks were safe for stepping on. Jared, a notorious follower in class, hesitated at the edge. "Ms. Tanner, are you sure this is safe?"

"Walk where I walk, Jared, and put your feet in my footsteps. I know what I'm doing, and I won't let you fall."

Later that afternoon, she sent Jared and another boy to fetch water, following them to ensure their safety. Over the rushing water, she heard Jared say, "Watch your step, Victor—water's deeper right there. I'll help you find where to step."

Claudia smiled. *Some leaders aren't born,* she thought. *They're made.*

Good leaders know when to exercise control. Too much, your students never make their learning their own; too little, they never respect what it is you're trying to teach them. God chose to give humans free will, knowing full well that people naturally tend not to walk in his footsteps. Just as God vies for your heart, however, you should also strive to set a godly example for your students.

Try this: *Arrange to attend a leadership workshop in your community. Make a list of leadership tips and begin to implement them one at a time in various areas of your life. The better your leadership skills, the more effective you will be at drawing out the leadership potential in your students.*

THE INTEGRITY OF THE UPRIGHT GUIDES THEM.

PROVERBS 11:3 NIV

REMEMBER YOUR LEADERS, WHO SPOKE THE WORD OF GOD TO YOU. CONSIDER THE OUTCOME OF THEIR WAY OF LIFE AND IMITATE THEIR FAITH.

HEBREWS 13:7 NIV

You must be careful how you walk, and where you go, for there are those following you who will set their feet where yours are set.

ROBERT E. LEE

Teacher of the Year

Let another praise you, and not your own mouth—a stranger, and not your own lips.

— *Proverbs* 27:2 NRSV

PRIDE IS TASTELESS, COLORLESS, AND SIZELESS. YET IT IS THE HARDEST THING TO SWALLOW.

AUGUST B. BLACK

Frank sat near the podium at the year-end assembly. A few of his seventh graders waved to him. He smiled and waved back. The principal, Sandy Dougherty, introduced him as the Teacher of the Year, and Frank stood briefly and nodded, and then sat back down. The applause continued and grew louder, and his students were standing. Sandy motioned for Frank to approach the microphone.

Frank felt the crimson burning at the back of his ears, the awkwardness of being singled out. He stepped up to the stand, shook Sandy's hand, and swallowed a hard lump in his throat. "I wasn't planning on speaking." He cleared his throat.

"Every day I work with all of you, future leaders—businesspeople, inventors, doctors, parents—and other talented and committed teachers. And every day, I'm a better person for it. I'm grateful for the privilege. Thank you."

✼ Few professions matter as much as teaching; still fewer have the potential for so little tangible recognition or reward. The beauty of teaching, however, is that you participate not only in God's plan for you but also in his designs for so many others. God has placed you in a position of great influence, making it important to stay humble. Praise God for using you in such a critical field, providing a voice of knowledge and wisdom to future generations.

✼ TRY THIS: *Find several definitions for the word pride. Then, study a situation—scientific discovery, short story, mathematical breakthrough—wherein one kind of pride or another factored in. Now consider a school situation where your pride has affected your agenda—in class, a staff meeting, or a parent conference. Jot down the particulars, and then write what you would do differently next time.*

PRIDE GOES BEFORE DESTRUCTION, AND A HAUGHTY SPIRIT BEFORE A FALL.

PROVERBS 16:18
NRSV

ALL MUST TEST THEIR OWN WORK; THEN THAT WORK, RATHER THAN THEIR NEIGHBOR'S WORK, WILL BECOME A CAUSE FOR PRIDE.

GALATIANS 6:4 NRSV

Be not proud of race, face, place or grace.
SAMUEL RUTHERFORD

The Trustworthy Teacher

I want to trust you, God divine,
But your love has late grown cold.
Can you not take hold my hand,
Before the day turns old?
Beloved one, My heart is there,
Showing but one sign:
For Me to help and take your hand,
First you must take Mine.

LEE EDWARD ROBERTS

A good name is more desirable than great riches.

~ *Proverbs* 22:1 NIV

You are a letter of Christ, cared for by us, written not with ink but with the Spirit of the living God, not on tablets of stone but on tablets of human hearts.

~ *2 Corinthians* 3:3 NASB

Confidence thrives on honesty, on honor, on the sacredness of obligations, on faithful protection and on unselfish performance. Without them it cannot live.

Franklin D. Roosevelt

Precious in His Sight

Speak up for those who cannot speak for themselves.

~ Proverbs 31:8 NIV

THE HEARTS OF
SMALL CHILDREN
ARE DELICATE
ORGANS. A CRUEL
BEGINNING IN
THIS WORLD CAN
TWIST THEM INTO
CURIOUS SHAPES.

CARSON MCCULLERS

As she watched Jenny stack chairs, Ann-Marie remembered why she had become a teacher. Bittersweet memories of her own childhood surfaced. She fondly remembered one of her teachers who had been there to listen when Ann-Marie could bear the pain of her parents' divorce no longer. Ann-Marie knew it was this teacher who had inspired her to love children and to be there to play a positive role in their lives.

Jenny was very much like Ann-Marie had been then, and her circumstances were similar. Jenny's father was gone, and she felt isolated from the other children by her pain. Jenny came to Ann-Marie's room at the day's end regularly to do simple chores and to spend a few moments in a safe haven. Ann-Marie often thanked God that he allowed her to provide that place for Jenny. Ann-Marie knew it was God's peace that attracted Jenny.

"Jenny, want to help me feed the hamster?" she asked, smiling.

There are few children who don't have some need, whether physical, mental, or emotional. As a teacher, you discharge a critical duty to prepare them for and protect them from the world they'll one day have to negotiate on their own. Recognizing each child's value is your primary privilege and responsibility as a teacher. You can help them to understand the value of their lives and the value of every human life.

Try this: Keep yourself open and alert to the needs of your children. Consider: Is their behavior age-appropriate? Has it changed since the beginning of the school year? Are their grades consistent? Be available to your students and pray that God will give you ears to listen and discernment to act.

THE NAME OF THE LORD IS A STRONG TOWER; THE RIGHTEOUS RUN TO IT AND ARE SAFE.

PROVERBS 18:10 NIV

DEFEND THE CAUSE OF THE WEAK AND THE FATHERLESS; MAINTAIN THE RIGHTS OF THE POOR AND OPPRESSED.

PSALM 82:3 NIV

God has sent children into the world, not only to replenish it, but to serve as sacred reminders of something ineffably precious which we are always in danger of losing.

ELTON TRUEBLOOD

The Master Teacher

Despise not the chastening of the LORD; neither be weary of his correction.

~ Proverbs 3:11 NRSV

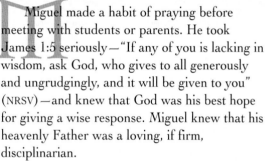

Correction is good when administered in time.

Author Unknown

Miguel made a habit of praying before meeting with students or parents. He took James 1:5 seriously—"If any of you is lacking in wisdom, ask God, who gives to all generously and ungrudgingly, and it will be given to you" (NRSV)—and knew that God was his best hope for giving a wise response. Miguel knew that his heavenly Father was a loving, if firm, disciplinarian.

"Jimmy," Miguel began, "we're all here today because I want us all on the same page before certain behaviors become bad habits." Jimmy nodded, relieved, and his parents' expressions brightened slightly. "You're here because you're a leader," Miguel continued. "That means you have two things—power and responsibility. It's a package deal. My question is, are you going to step up and be that leader?"

Jimmy's dad approached Miguel afterward. "He thinks he's a bad kid, but you called him a leader. That kind of confidence goes a long way."

As a teacher, you need to remember the lessons you've learned from God in establishing your own corrective procedures. Without dropping scriptures on students and parents, let the wisdom therein inform your own correctional techniques in terms of consistency, justice and charity. This is a sure sign of God's sanctifying work in your life. Search for verses that demonstrate both God's resolve in punishing sin and his grace in forgiving it.

Try this: Create a contract for yourself as a teacher regarding your expectations for your conduct and standards, and what your students and colleagues can expect from you. Sign and post it in a visible place in your room. Encourage students to point out, gently, times when you violate it. Measure your response carefully; you're still the adult, but accountability earns respect.

God will be glorified in the punishment of sin as well as in the reward of obedience.

THOMAS V. MOORE

Idle Words

Do not associate with a gossip.

— *Proverbs 20:19* NASB

WHOEVER
GOSSIPS TO YOU
WILL GOSSIP
OF YOU.

AUTHOR UNKNOWN

Geraldine had been a teacher for forty-three years, and the single guarantee she repeatedly made to students and colleagues was that gossip was a surefire poison for school morale. She had a reputation for being the last person anyone would want to include in the gossip grapevine. A recently transferred teacher discovered this the hard way.

Attempting to ingratiate herself with Geraldine, the staff's senior member, the new teacher attempted to fill Geraldine in on the rather scandalous details surrounding her transfer. Geraldine listened for a few minutes until the unfortunate newcomer dropped the name of her previous school's principal and insinuated a shady relationship with key board members.

Geraldine's reaction was as quick as it was calm. "Is that so? Why don't I call him and hear what he has to say about that." She pulled her cell phone out of her handbag. "Let's see if he's at work now."

You can never underestimate the power of hearsay—in its wake kingdoms rise and fall. As a Christian and as a teacher, you need to watch for rumors carefully. Not only is there a biblical injunction to shun gossip, but there is also the added danger of succumbing to good intentions. Pray for the wisdom to find your balance being a trustworthy listener and being a gossip.

RASH WORDS ARE LIKE SWORD THRUSTS, BUT THE TONGUE OF THE WISE BRINGS HEALING.

PROVERBS 12:18 NRSV

TRY THIS: *Remind yourself how the classic game "telephone" goes—remember that it doesn't take much to garble ordinary facts into something that is not only untrue but is crazy. Consider suggesting this game for your next in-service training as a reminder to participants that the best communication technique is always one-to-one.*

WITHOUT WOOD A FIRE GOES OUT; WITHOUT GOSSIP A QUARREL DIES DOWN.

PROVERBS 26:20 NIV

Never listen to accounts of the frailties of others; and if anyone should complain to you of another, humbly ask him not to speak of him at all.

SAINT JOHN OF THE CROSS

Highly Recommended

To be highly respected is better than having silver or gold.

~ *Proverbs 22:1 NIrV*

IT IS BETTER TO
BE ALONE THAN
IN BAD
COMPANY.

GEORGE
WASHINGTON

Todd knocked on Tammy's door and poked his head in. "Mrs. Trujillo? I just wanted to drop by and tell you thanks. I heard your letter of recommendation made all the difference."

Tammy grinned. "You're welcome, Todd. It was the easiest letter I've ever had to write. Just being who you are, and working as hard as you do, spoke for itself." They spoke for several more minutes, Todd explaining his new bus route across town to the science academy, and Tammy providing the names of some trustworthy contacts.

Finally, Todd stood to leave. "You know, Mrs. Trujillo, you wrote some really nice things about me." He smiled confidently. "I appreciate the opportunity, and I'll be sure not to disappoint your trust in me or let either of us down."

When you are teaching, you do not simply represent yourself at school; you also represent God. Rather than feeling pressured because of that fact, you should actually feel relief, and even joy, at the prospect that all you say and do is emblematic of the almighty Creator of the universe, whose love for you has been demonstrated in the highest manner possible. When your standards of conduct are God's, you want to keep the family name pure and proud.

TRY THIS: *Write about your reputation. Start with how you think others see you now, and how you see yourself. Then project yourself five or ten years into the future and write what you would want people to be able to say about you then. What present attitudes and habits would have to change?*

A GOOD REPUTATION IS BETTER THAN EXPENSIVE PERFUME.

ECCLESIASTES 7:1
GNT

DO NOT BE MISLED: "BAD COMPANY CORRUPTS GOOD CHARACTER."

1 CORINTHIANS 15:33
NIV

A reputation once broken may possibly be repaired, but the world will always keep their eyes on the spot where the crack was.

JOSEPH HALL

The Loving Teacher

Joy is love exalted;

Peace is love in repose;

Long-suffering is love enduring;

Gentleness is love in society;

Goodness is love in action;

Faith is love on the battlefield;

Meekness is love in school;

And temperance is love in training.

D. L. Moody

Let love and faithfulness never leave you.

~ *Proverbs* 3:3 NIV

May the Lord make your love increase and overflow for each other and for everyone else.

~ *1 Thessalonians* 3:12 NIV

When I have learnt to love God better than my earthly dearest, I shall love my earthly dearest better than I do now.

C. S. Lewis

Doing All Things

The way of the LORD is strength to the upright.

— *Proverbs* 10:29 KJV

Carmen watched her basketball team get off the bus. The first student off, as always, was Kimberly. She fairly bounced with pent-up energy. Carmen turned to her assistant coach, Jamie, and said, "Have you ever seen anything like it?"

Jamie shook her head admiringly. "Coaches dream of having leaders like her, and she's the same way in my journalism class." Jamie leaned in as they followed the girls into the gym. Her eyes were still on Kimberly. "I guess it's in remission now?" she asked.

"Yes—and you'd never guess she'd been sick," Carmen chuckled. "And you know who she credits for her attitude, don't you? God. She says he's given her eagle's wings. What do you think about that?"

Jamie caught her friend's eye and smiled. "Well, it sure wasn't the leukemia that gave her back to us, was it?"

A wise athlete—one who trains consistently and plans strategy—always has an advantage over a stronger but unmindful opponent. The courageous and careful general of a smaller army always makes life difficult for a brutish army of larger numbers. No matter what challenges you face at school—huge class sizes, few resources, troubled students—God will give you the strength to stand. In fact, only in God will you find the strength necessary to face them all.

TRY THIS: *Read one or two biographies of people who, through God's power and grace, overcame great odds and struggles to achieve success. Suggestions include John Bunyan, John Wycliffe, Amy Carmichael, Corrie ten Boom. Describe the obstacles each faced, and how each found the strength to overcome adversity and opposition.*

THOSE WHO HOPE IN THE LORD WILL RENEW THEIR STRENGTH.

ISAIAH 40:31 NIV

I CAN DO ALL THINGS THROUGH CHRIST WHICH STRENGTHENETH ME.

PHILIPPIANS 4:13 KJV

We are not weak enough. It is not our strength that we want. One drop of God's strength is worth more than all the world.

D. L. MOODY

A Little Common Sense

Preserve sound judgment and discernment.

~ Proverbs 3:21 NIV

Ron watched the situation develop from across the library. He knew Marc well enough to know what was going through his mind. Marc, an antsy eighth grader, had a chalk-filled eraser in hand and seemed to be weighing the entertainment value of dusting the back of the girl working next to him. His eyes twinkled mischievously. Ron knew that Marc was aware that one more offense, no matter how minor, would result in an in-house suspension. Marc was a decent kid who just let his sense of humor sway his good judgment. Good sense just got away from him at times.

Ron had talked to Marc numerous times about his actions. *Hesitate before making a choice, Marc. Consider the consequences.* Ron pursed his lip, waiting.

Marc stood motionless for a second, glanced around him, and then returned the eraser to the chalk shelf. On the way back to his desk, he caught Ron's eye and. Ron smiled back.

Take every opportunity to help your students realize the importance of making solid, practical, morally reasoned choices. Kids struggle to understand that their actions have consequences. Make sure that in your class good behaviors are rewarded and poor behaviors have realistic outcomes. Every lesson, from initial directions to lectures to activities and final products can teach students how their choices affect themselves and others.

Try this: Make a list of five rules for your personal conduct. Describe how those factors affect the way you treat people—older, younger, peers, different social classes, ethnicities, or religions, especially where it pertains to your students and coworkers. Number the points and, for the next week, consciously assess how well you measure up to your own standards.

Jesus said, "Stop judging by mere appearances, and make a right judgment."

John 7:24 NIV

The Lord said, "I will deal with them according to their conduct, and by their own standards I will judge them."

Ezekiel 7:27 NIV

Common sense is compelled to make its way without the enthusiasm of anyone; all admit it grudgingly.

EDGAR WATSON HOWE

Let God Do It

Commit your works to the LORD, and your plans will be established.

~ Proverbs 16:3 NASB

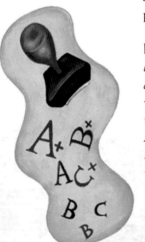

Kendall tossed and turned that night, wrestling with her thoughts. She usually left school at school so that she could give her family the attention they deserved. That way she could go back refreshed on the next day.

Tonight, however, she couldn't quit thinking about one particular student—a girl who was having to deal with a destructive home situation. She seemed beyond Kendall's ability to help, and the fruitlessness of Kendall's appeals to the principal to do something plagued her sleep

Finally Kendall slipped out of bed and onto her knees. *Lord, what can I do? I can't get through to this girl. Why can't I do anything? Do I not care enough?* Kendall's feelings poured out of her, with little relief at first. Finally some quiet thoughts came to her. *Just love the girl, Kendall. Accept the situation. God is sovereign. He will teach her through you. Just let him.* Kendall's heart flooded with peace.

Teachers need to retain a certain emotional distance from students to preserve sanity. Nevertheless, you do begin to care about your students, and you sometimes struggle to find appropriate ways to help them with the difficulties in their lives. Sometimes you can help and sometimes you cannot. When the latter is true, give those situations to the God. He may help you see that you've overlooked a potential solution. More important, he will give you peace that your student is safe in his care.

Try this: *At home, keep a list of students you wish to pray for. Be sure to update the list with a short explanation when you see God's hand moving in that student's life or you find that God has inspired you with a potential solution you can offer the student in regard to a specific problem.*

Jesus said, "Yet not as I will, but as you will."

Matthew 26:39 NIV

The human mind may devise many plans, but it is the purpose of the Lord that will be established.

Proverbs 19:21 NRSV

Our satisfaction lies in submission to the divine embrace.

Jan Van Ruysbroeck

Taking Care of Yourself

Do not be wise in your own eyes; fear the Lord and shun evil. This will bring health to your body and nourishment to your bones.

~ *Proverbs 3:7–8 NIV*

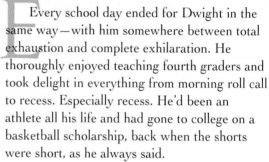

TAKE CARE OF YOUR HEALTH, THAT IT MAY SERVE YOU TO SERVE GOD.

SAINT FRANCIS OF SALES

Every school day ended for Dwight in the same way—with him somewhere between total exhaustion and complete exhilaration. He thoroughly enjoyed teaching fourth graders and took delight in everything from morning roll call to recess. Especially recess. He'd been an athlete all his life and had gone to college on a basketball scholarship, back when the shorts were short, as he always said.

Inevitably his students would discover his history as a "famous" player after he rained a few thirty-foot jumpers down on them at recess. This would generally lead to such questions as, "Gosh, Mr. Phelps, they had basketball back when you were in college?" or "How come you're still so good, Mr. Phelps?"

Dwight would smile, ruffle someone's hair, and give his usual answer. "Two reasons, kids: clean living and God's grace. You don't survive twenty-six years of teaching fourth graders without good health and divine intervention."

The business of teaching exacts a powerful toll on your mind, your body, and on your spiritual life. You're at your best when you replenish all three aspects, and you'll need to make sure you do this every day. Take care of yourself: cultivate other interests besides teaching; eat well, exercise, and talk to God. God promises to equip you for every good work. It is up to you to take responsibility for maintaining the instrument he uses—you.

Try this: Log your eating and exercise habits for a week and analyze your logs for nutritional content and activity. Determine which foods help you to feel and perform at your highest levels. In a similar diary, track what you do for entertainment—what type of books, TV shows, movies, games. Consider how these choices affect your mental and emotional well-being.

HE WILL RENEW YOUR LIFE AND SUSTAIN YOU IN YOUR OLD AGE.

RUTH 4:15 NIV

THE LORD SAID, "FOR AS THE DAYS OF A TREE, SO WILL BE THE DAYS OF MY PEOPLE; MY CHOSEN ONES WILL LONG ENJOY THE WORKS OF THEIR HANDS."

ISAIAH 65:22 NIV

The secret of the physical well-being of the Christian is the vitality of the divine life welling up within by virtue of his incorporation into Christ.

EVELYN FROST

The Faithful Teacher

In order to arrive at having pleasure

in everything,

Desire to have pleasure in nothing.

In order to arrive at possessing everything,

Desire to possess nothing.

In order to arrive at being everything,

Desire to be nothing.

In order to arrive at knowing everything,

Desire to know nothing.

Saint John of the Cross

The faithful will abound with blessings.

~ *Proverbs* 28:20 NRSV

We walk by faith, not by sight.

~ *2 Corinthians* 5:7 KJV

I long to accomplish a great and noble task, but it is my chief duty to accomplish small tasks as they were great and noble.

HELEN KELLER

Listen Up

God said, "Now, my children, listen to me, and be attentive to the words of my mouth."

— *Proverbs* 7:24 NRSV

THINK LIKE A WISE MAN BUT COMMUNICATE IN THE LANGUAGE OF THE PEOPLE.

W. B. YEATS

Vicki looked from the paper to the boy's eyes and back. She was scanning his work while trying to think of what connection she could make based on his interests and understanding. She threw up a quick prayer for wisdom.

She had experience—eight years now—and skill, having seen just about every conceivable variety of writer and level of ability possible at the sixth grade level. Each child held a unique story of his or her life, and that's what she wanted to get at.

"I noticed that your story is about bike racing, Stephen." The boy bobbed his head. "You have lots of good details here, but what I want to know is, how do you feel when you're racing?" Stephen's eyes flickered, and suddenly the words came tumbling out in his descriptions of the adrenaline, the tension, and the potential danger of the berms and blacktops. "Stephen, stop. You've got it. Now go write it."

Listening is crucial to communication. Paul's primary method of winning people to Christ was to be sensitive to their needs and identify with them. Your best opportunities to get through to your students will come when you reach them where they are today and expect to see results later. Instead of checking your store of ready answers, try to hear what students are saying so that your words address their specific concerns.

Try this: *Keep a notebook and jot down key points from what others say in meetings. Then, when they're finished, and you begin to address their concerns, start by saying, "If I understood you correctly" or "What I'm hearing from you is . . ." By doing this, you can immediately clarify any misunderstandings and show that you want what's best for everyone.*

To draw near to listen is better than the sacrifice offered by fools.

Ecclesiastes 5:1
NRSV

I have become all things to all men, so that I may by all means save some.

I Corinthians 9:22
NASB

When God wants to speak and deal with us, he does not avail himself of an angel but of parents, or the pastor, or of our neighbor.

Martin Luther

Continuing Education

Let the wise listen and add to their learning.
— *Proverbs 1:5* NIV

One's mind is like a knife. If you don't sharpen it, it gets rusty.

Nien Ching

Cleo was happy to be back in the classroom at the beginning of the term. She'd spent two weeks during the summer taking an online course on teaching character through film, and she prayed her students would respond to the unit she'd created from it. Sure enough, when she described the unit to her class, they replied "All right!" "Let's get started now!"—a real achievement coming from sophomores.

"This is going to be so great, Mrs. Rico," said Belinda. "I've always wanted to make a film."

"Right," agreed Cleo. "I know what you mean, because that's exactly how I felt in my class this summer."

"Wait a minute," said Thomas. "You took a class? In the summer? But you're a teacher! Why would you have to go to class?"

Cleo laughed. "It's a fast-paced world, and you're fast-paced kids. My goal is to be a better teacher every year than I was the year before."

One of teaching's great joys is that you are constantly learning—about various subjects, about human nature, about yourself as a learner, and about God's grace. It's a tremendous gift to pass on your status as a lifelong learner to your students. Your attitude as a teacher should reflect the high goal of knowing God more and better. Acts 7:22 describes Moses as being educated in Egyptian wisdom and speech, and yet he was barely at the beginning of God's plan for him.

Try this: Model the work that you require of your students. When you ask them to journal, journal with them; when they have a science fair project, do one yourself. It's hard to find the time for this—you're busy enough—but when your students see you as a learner, it inspires them more than your words alone.

GIVE INSTRUCTION TO THE WISE, AND THEY WILL BECOME WISER STILL; TEACH THE RIGHTEOUS AND THEY WILL GAIN IN LEARNING.

PROVERBS 9:9 NRSV

PAUL SAID, "CONTINUE IN WHAT YOU HAVE LEARNED AND FIRMLY BELIEVED, KNOWING FROM WHOM YOU LEARNED IT."

2 TIMOTHY 3:14 NRSV

One of the reasons mature people stop learning is that they become less and less willing to risk failure.

JOHN GARDNER

WORD TO THE WISE

The wise listen to advice.

— *Proverbs 12:15 NRSV*

TO PROFIT FROM GOOD ADVICE REQUIRES MORE WISDOM THAN TO GIVE IT.

JOHN CHURTON COLLINS

Gwen sat at her desk, the students gone for the day, her mind swimming with thoughts and questions. She had gone all out to organize the science fair, but she'd had to do most of the work herself. *Why had the other teachers opted not to help?* she wondered.

"Hi there," said Janine, sticking her head in the door. "Great job on the science fair." Gwen looked up at her colleague. Janine had been the one who had quietly guided her through many first-year teaching pitfalls.

"You think so?" she responded. "Thanks. I'm glad it all worked out, but it would have been nice if someone had offered to help."

"I'm sure they were waiting for you to ask," Janine said, pulling up a chair. "Unless you tell them, they have no way of knowing what you need. Next time, let them know—specifically."

"Thanks, Janine, Gwen responded. "That's excellent advice."

100

Giving or receiving advice can be tricky. Words that are too frank can cut deeply, while words that dance around the heart of an issue come across as trite and superficial. If you're giving advice, the best strategy is to listen before speaking and to put yourself in the other person's place. If you're on the receiving end, seek out advice before you begin a new project.

Try this: *Write down the best piece of educational advice a fellow teacher ever gave you. Describe why it helped at the time and also how it has helped you improve as a teacher and as a person since then. Now write down the one piece of advice (besides the previous one) that you would give to a teacher just starting out.*

Advice is like snow; the softer it falls, the longer it dwells upon, and the deeper it sinks into the mind.

Samuel Taylor Coleridge

How Great Thou Art

The fear of the LORD is the beginning of knowledge.

~ *Proverbs 1:7 NASB*

GOD TRULY IS,
BECAUSE HE IS
UNCHANGEABLE.

SAINT AUGUSTINE
OF HIPPO

After class, Patty sat down with the principal, Dr. Smith, and the two representatives from the State Board who had been invited to observe her class as part of the school's improvement plan. They were impressed with the quality of the students' work, Patty's clear and easy-to-understand instruction, and her easy, caring rapport with all the students in her class.

Dr. Smith noted that these were among the reasons why he had chosen Patty's class for observation, along with her ability to imbue even the most routine tasks with meaning beyond their surface value. "It's as if you have angels on your shoulders guiding your every footstep," he chuckled.

When asked what her strategy was, Patty explained her approach, and added with a mysterious smile, "Actually, I'm used to being observed; I approach every day with the idea that I'm working under the gaze of the Person whose opinion I value most."

What a privilege as a teacher, not only to be in a position to do so much good for so many people, but also to live and move and teach with the knowledge that God is always with you. As you grow in your relationship with Jesus, you appreciate more and more his nearness, his work all around you and in you. Time spent reading your Bible, praying, and worshiping1 draws you closer to God and enables you to recognize his presence.

Try this: Resolve to recognize God at work "incognito" around your school. In your journal, log all of the situations and incidents that others might call coincidence or luck, but that you know must be the working of your loving Father. At the top, write GOD IS NOT SILENT; I MUST LEARN TO LISTEN. Try to add one new entry each day.

FOR A DAY IN YOUR COURTS IS BETTER THAN A THOUSAND ELSEWHERE.

PSALM 84:10 NRSV

DRAW NEAR TO GOD, AND HE WILL DRAW NEAR TO YOU.

JAMES 4:8 NRSV

We may ignore, but we can nowhere evade, the presence of God. The world is crowded with him. He walks everywhere incognito.

C. S. LEWIS

The Cheerful Teacher

Joy is the wine that

God is ever pouring

Into the hearts of those

who strive with Him,

Lighting their eye to vision and airing,

Strengthening their arms to warfare

glad and grim.

G. A. Studdert Kennedy

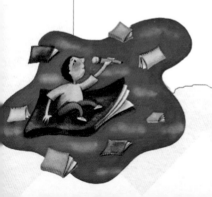

*A happy heart makes
the face cheerful.*
~ *Proverbs 15:13* NIV

Be joyful always.
~ *1 Thessalonians 5:16* NIV

REAL JOY COMES
NOT FROM EASE OR
RICHES OR FROM
PRAISE OF MEN,
BUT FROM DOING
SOMETHING
WORTHWHILE.

SIR WILFRED GRENFELL

Please Find a Seat

A cheerful look brings joy to the heart.
— Proverbs 15:30 NIV

When the senior humanities students entered their classroom on the first day of school, they found Randolph, their teacher, dressed in a black tuxedo. He stood by a pyramid of plastic champagne flutes that were arranged on a white-cloth covered table at the back.

"Come in, come in!" he encouraged cheerily. He pulled a two-liter bottle of lemon-lime soda from a cooler and dramatically poured it in a cascade over the flutes. "Welcome to the first day of the rest of your life." On the board behind him the students saw this message: IT BEGINS TODAY, SENIORS, AND IT BEGINS WITH YOU!

"Mr. Harmon?" ventured one student. "What's going on?"

"A toast, my young charges: this whole year is a celebration, of many things. Come every day as you came today—as you are, eager, and perhaps scared and perhaps joyous—and it will be a year worth celebrating."

What would it be like if you were a student in your classroom—did the teacher say "Hi" or "Good morning"? Did she take the time to ask about your dad's job interview or your grandmother's health? Were you glad you came that day, because you knew you'd be in a safe place, learning some important things? It's easy to get so busy that you forget that your kids are counting on you to make school worthwhile.

TRY THIS: *Arrange a special event on a day when your students least expect it, perhaps the first day of school, the first day back from a holiday, or some random Tuesday. Think of special things in your life that have made you feel welcome—a surprise party, a little note, a daily chore found completed—and make those things happen for your kids.*

Kind words are the music of the world. They have a power which seems to be beyond natural causes.

FREDERICK WILLIAM FABER

It's the Right Thing

The integrity of the upright shall guide them.

— *Proverbs* 11:3 *KJV*

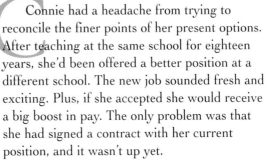

Connie had a headache from trying to reconcile the finer points of her present options. After teaching at the same school for eighteen years, she'd been offered a better position at a different school. The new job sounded fresh and exciting. Plus, if she accepted she would receive a big boost in pay. The only problem was that she had signed a contract with her current position, and it wasn't up yet.

She heard the words of colleagues, close friends, and parents echoing in her head. "You're a teacher—you've got to take the money when you can." "I'd love to have the opportunity you have before you."

Connie prayed, asking God to help her sort through it all and find the right answer. Finally she said to the recruiters, "You've been very kind, but I signed a contract, and I intend to keep it. Besides, I can't leave those kids, I love them too much." Her headache went away moments later.

Integrity is the byword for teachers, partly because it has to be—who goes into education for the money?—and partly because it ought to be—who other than parents has greater influence in young people's lives? More than most other professionals, you know that what you do has an impact on the future, and that should give you plenty of reasons to be sure that your actions and words are right and good.

TRY THIS: *List the times when upholding your integrity has cost you something, in terms of social or financial status. Now list the times that God has blessed you—perhaps short term, perhaps in the long run—for staying true to him. How do your lists compare? Do the results surprise you?*

LET INTEGRITY AND UPRIGHTNESS PRESERVE ME, FOR I WAIT ON THEE.

PSALM 25:21 KJV

SHOW YOURSELF IN ALL RESPECTS A MODEL OF GOOD WORKS, AND IN YOUR TEACHING SHOW INTEGRITY.

TITUS 2:7 NRSV

Integrity is the glue that holds our way of life together.
BILLY GRAHAM

A Sense of Satisfaction

Happy are those who find wisdom, and those who get understanding.

~ *Proverbs 3:13* NRSV

FULFILLMENT OF YOUR DESTINY DOES NOT COME IN A MOMENT, A MONTH, OR A YEAR, BUT OVER A LIFETIME.

CASEY TREAT

Charlie was fascinated. He had been watching Colleen run her classroom all morning. He was there as an observer and was getting ready to begin his student teaching. He hadn't seen anyone like Colleen before. She seemed to be completely aware of her students' needs and abilities. Charlie watched as she gave brief, deft advice to one student and then walked across the room to intervene in a conversation that was headed from civilized to ugly. *Wow,* he marveled. *How does she do all of this?*

At lunch, he asked her. "It's hard work," Colleen replied, "but I don't mind because I know I'm doing what God has called me to do. I'm using the gifts and abilities he has given me."

Charlie nodded; he had respect for the results he had seen. Colleen continued. "Doing what you were created to do provides a sense of fulfillment that can't be obtained any other way."

110

Pause for a moment and thank God for putting you in a place where you can fulfill his plan for your life. He has given you all the gifts and abilities you need to inspire and motivate the next generation. Take satisfaction in the fact that you are busy doing what God has called you to do and that you're doing it well. No amount of money or status could provide the sense of fulfillment you have as a teacher.

Try this: *What in your life truly fulfills you? List those activities or beliefs that your life would be much poorer without. Describe how God uses those items on your list to work out his plans for your life. Consider the fruit of the Spirit (Galatians 5:22–23), and check your list to see if what's there matches up with God's will for you.*

BLESSED ARE THEY WHICH DO HUNGER AND THIRST AFTER RIGHTEOUSNESS: FOR THEY SHALL BE FILLED.

MATTHEW 5:6 KJV

THE LORD WILL FULFILL HIS PURPOSE FOR ME; YOUR LOVE, O LORD, ENDURES FOREVER—DO NOT ABANDON THE WORKS OF YOUR HANDS.

PSALM 138:8 NIV

Find satisfaction in him who made you, and only then find satisfaction in yourself as part of his creation.

SAINT AUGUSTINE OF HIPPO

That's How It Goes

Some friends play at friendship but a true friend sticks closer than one's nearest kin.

~ *Proverbs 18:24* NRSV

Tim waited for the boy's tears to subside. This was one of the hardest parts of teaching middle schoolers—helping them with the realization that the guys they thought would be their friends until they were old and gray weren't actually going to be their friends even until tomorrow. *Take James here*, he thought. *At the start of the year, he and Malcolm were inseparable; now, Malcolm started a rumor about James, and James is crushed.*

"It won't help you to keep asking why he did it. You may never really know why." James looked up at Tim through his tears. "So keep looking for the people out there who appreciate you for being you," Tim continued. "You're a good and trustworthy friend. I can think of at least five guys who'd love to have a friend like you."

James nodded. Tim smiled. "It hurts now, but it'll feel better soon."

When you're teaching you usually needn't stop to consider your influences. And yet you know you never do anything entirely by yourself—you're a product of your own education, upbringing, and relationships. That's why it is crucial to have at least one true friend, one who lifts your spirits just by being there, one who is able to shoot straight with you when no one else can or will. In order to have a friend like that, you must first be a friend like that.

TRY THIS: *Study some of the Bible's true friendships—Ruth and Naomi, David and Jonathan, Paul and Barnabas. Consider what made those friendships successful: Who took the initiative and why? Who made promises and kept them? How was God a factor? Applying this wisdom, cultivate a friendship at school; pray that God would reveal the right person and help you to be a good friend.*

FAITHFUL ARE THE WOUNDS OF A FRIEND; BUT THE KISSES OF AN ENEMY ARE DECEITFUL.

PROVERBS 27:6 KJV

WHOEVER WALKS WITH THE WISE BECOMES WISE, BUT THE COMPANION OF FOOLS SUFFERS HARM.

PROVERBS 13:20 NRSV

A true friend can never have a hidden motive for being a friend. He can have no hidden agenda. A friend is simply a friend, for the sake of friendship.

JAMES HOUSTON

The Attentive Teacher

'Twas only when I stopped my speaking

that my ears did hear. . . .

'Twas only when I stopped to help

that I did change my views. . . .

Now I live, your light inside,

to glorify your name.

S. Scott Summers

The LORD has given us eyes to see with and ears to listen with.

~ *Proverbs 20:12* GNT

Each of you should look not only to your own interests, but also to the interests of others.

~ *Philippians 2:4* NIV

A LITTLE CONSIDERATION, A LITTLE THOUGHT FOR OTHERS, MAKES ALL THE DIFFERENCE.

A. A. MILNE

GOD IS ON YOUR SIDE

There is no wisdom, no insight, no plan that can succeed against the LORD.

~ *Proverbs 21:30* NIV

Christopher shook his head, comparing the four essays in front of him, his initial disbelief changing to disappointment and then to muted fury. Cheating on their final exam? How could they make such a stupid mistake? The red wave of anger receded and another, calmer influence took over. Chris closed his eyes to pray. *Father, these are four of my best students, but what they've done goes against everything I thought they stood for. What should I do?*

There was nothing easy about Christopher's meeting with the students and their parents. All four students were suspended according to school policy for cheating; the evidence had been undeniable.

Chris spoke with them afterward. Firmly but gently, his heart reached out to them. "You need to know something: Your decision to cheat has brought trouble into your lives, but that trouble has a purpose. It is intended to make you wiser in the future. Make it work for you."

116

How you face trouble depends on what you do with it. You can languish in it and feel sorry for yourself. You can rise up against it and feel angry and bitter. Or you can use it and learn from what you're going through. As a teacher, you'll be asked to deal with trouble on a daily basis. It may be the consequence of your poor choice or the poor choices of others. Either way, how you deal with these choices will make the difference.

GOD IS OUR REFUGE AND STRENGTH, A VERY PRESENT HELP IN TROUBLE.

PSALM 46:1 KJV

TRY THIS: *Develop a crisis response itinerary. Consider different levels of trouble — school-related, community, national, and international. When things happen on each level, how will you respond? Where will your focus be? What perspective will you offer your students in each situation? Write down your responses. Be prepared for trouble by knowing where you stand as a Christian educator.*

THIS SMALL AND TEMPORARY TROUBLE WE SUFFER WILL BRING US A TREMENDOUS AND ETERNAL GLORY, MUCH GREATER THAN THE TROUBLE.

2 CORINTHIANS 4:17 GNT

The meaning of earthly existence lies, not as we have grown used to thinking, in prospering, but in the development of the soul.

ALEXANDER SOLZHENITSYN

Making the Mark

The plans of people who work hard succeed.

— *Proverbs 21:5 NIRV*

Dave was determined to find a way to encourage his students to be enthusiastic about the term papers they were required to do. One morning as he was preparing for the day, he had a thought. Why not let them do some original research and collect fresh data from their peers?

The next day, he explained his new approach to the class, and next week, Dave's students polled their fellow high schoolers in several classes to learn new areas of interest. When they had come up with an assortment of interesting ideas, they broadened their typical library research by calling on local businesses, agencies, and other professionals who could offer insight and information for their papers.

Dave was gratified by the happy buzz of busy, purposeful students. Each student seemed eager to uncover some deeper truth about their corner of the world. Proudly he told them, "You have learned how to make a week seven todays instead of seven tomorrows."

While it's important for you to establish routines for your students, it's also important that you always strive to improve the quality of their learning. Diligence is the by-product both of patience and creativity, staying true to your calling on the one hand, but never fearing to sing the new song that God gives you (Psalm 40). Set your mind to work finding new ways to draw your students into a positive learning experience rather than settling for "just another assignment."

Try this: *List the things that make teaching difficult for you—parent-teacher conferences, grading, doing report cards, meetings—whatever they are. Put these as headings on index cards in a card box. When you read or hear a tip or interesting idea for dealing with any of those items, write it down on a card and place it in the box.*

Let us run with perseverance the race marked out for us.

Hebrews 12:1 NIV

Whatever your task, put yourselves into it, as done for the Lord and not for your masters.

Colossians 3:23 NRSV

All labor that uplifts humanity has dignity and importance and should be undertaken with painstaking excellence.

Martin Luther King Jr.

It Can Be Fixed

Love covereth all sins.

— *Proverbs 10:12 KJV*

"I can forgive but I cannot forget," is only another way of saying, "I cannot forgive."

HENRY WARD BEECHER

Wanda had spent the last thirty minutes trying to help two students resolve an ongoing conflict. She had appealed to their sense of maturity as eighth graders as well as to the need for them to take responsibility for making things right.

Her head was throbbing, but Wanda continued to lead them along. "Jenny, you say, 'Eddie, when you do this, I feel like this.' Eddie, you say, 'Jenny, when you do this, I feel like this.'" With her guidance, the responses became more specific and eventually led to unprompted apologies.

Wanda breathed a quick prayer of thanks. "That's better! Don't you two forget that you're pretty good friends and that you like a lot of things about each other."

"Good friendships take work—you should each be looking for the first opportunity to forgive each other and make things right." Jenny and Eddie left happy, and Wanda went happily for a headache tablet.

Forgiveness is the oil that keeps the machinery of communication functioning at peak efficiency. You've needed to receive it and you've needed to give it—and probably you're needed for both on most days. A simple apology, even when sincere, can never replace the value of true forgiveness, which puts the ball in the court of the offended party, making it the only real way to set things aright.

Try this: Keep a forgiveness ledger for one week. In two sets of columns, record OFFENSES GIVEN AND FORGIVENESS SOUGHT/RECEIVED and OFFENSES RECEIVED AND FORGIVENESS GIVEN. Work to "clear" each account as appropriate. Once you've either sought and received forgiveness or offered it for offenses taken, black it out with a permanent marker.

HE WHO COVERS OVER AN OFFENSE PROMOTES LOVE.

PROVERBS 17:9 NIV

BEAR WITH EACH OTHER AND FORGIVE WHATEVER GRIEVANCES YOU MAY HAVE AGAINST ONE ANOTHER. FORGIVE AS THE LORD FORGAVE YOU.

COLOSSIANS 3:13 NIV

When you forgive, you in no way change the past—but you sure do change the future.

BERNARD MELTZER

Just a Coincidence?

All our steps are ordered by the LORD.

— *Proverbs 20:24* NRSV

THE WILL OF
GOD WILL
NEVER TAKE YOU
WHERE THE
GRACE OF GOD
CANNOT KEEP
YOU.

AUTHOR
UNKNOWN

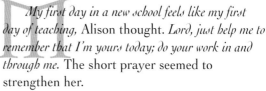

My first day in a new school feels like my first day of teaching, Alison thought. *Lord, just help me to remember that I'm yours today; do your work in and through me.* The short prayer seemed to strengthen her.

She held open the door for a small boy who thanked her and walked confidently inside. She saw him twice more that day—he was a student in her third-period calculus class, and then she saw him waiting for his ride in the parking lot after school. "Hi, Sam," she said cheerfully. "Seeing you again makes me feel like I've made a friend on my first day here."

Sam looked surprised. "It's my first day too! What's funny is that I came here to take calculus—your class! My school didn't have it, and they said they had an expert here." Alison's heart leaped as the tumblers clicked into place. *There are no accidents with you, are there, Father?*

One of the most dangerous things a Christian can do is to diminish God, to make him anything less than completely sovereign, omnipotent, omniscient, and omnipresent. In this day of the spiritual-buffet mentality, you can give no quarter here. God's presence and his plan will comfort you. Your students, colleagues, and administrators will all benefit daily from working with someone whose every step is carefully placed in God's hands.

TRY THIS: *Leave space in your daily planner to record the work that God will do each day. Pray that he will help you to perceive him at work in your life and in the lives you touch. Seeing God's plan in writing as you recognize it, even if only partially, will help develop an appreciation for your Father's attention to detail.*

THE PLANS OF THE LORD STAND FIRM FOREVER, THE PURPOSES OF HIS HEART THROUGH ALL GENERATIONS.

PSALM 33:11 NIV

IN HIM WE WERE ALSO CHOSEN, HAVING BEEN PREDESTINED ACCORDING TO THE PLAN OF HIM WHO WORKS OUT EVERYTHING IN CONFORMITY WITH THE PURPOSE OF HIS WILL.

EPHESIANS 1:11 NIV

Inside the will of God there is no failure. Outside the will of God there is no success.

BENARD EDINGER

The Humble Teacher

Small service is true service while it lasts:

Of humblest friends, bright creature,

scorn not one:

The daisy, by the shadow that it casts,

Protects the lingering dew-drop

from the sun.

William Wordsworth

By humility and the fear of the LORD are riches, and honour, and life.

~ *Proverbs* 22:4 KJV

Jesus said, "All who exalt themselves will be humbled, and those who humble themselves will be exalted."

~ *Luke* 14:11 NRSV

To be humble to superiors, is duty; to equals, is courtesy; to inferiors, is nobleness; and to all, safety; it being a virtue that, for all its lowliness, commandeth those it stoops to.

Sir Thomas More

At Inspirio we love to hear from you—your
stories, your feedback,
and your product ideas.
Please send your comments to us
by way of e-mail at
icares@zondervan.com
or to the address below:

inspirio

Attn: Inspirio Cares
5300 Patterson Avenue SE
Grand Rapids, MI 49530

If you would like further information
about Inspirio and the products we
create please visit us at:
www.inspiriogifts.com

Thank you and God Bless!